Satanique Magique

books 1, 2, & 3-GREED, VANITY, & ENVY

Dedication...

I dedicate this book to anyone who seeks to overcome feeling guilt for seeking pleasure and self fulfilment, for self admiration and self appreciation, & for admiring what others have and wanting it for themselves as well.

This paperback includes the first 3 'sins'....GREED, VANITY, & ENVY........and 'HELLthy QUEER Creating-sigils for empowerment'

about this series...

Each of the '7 deadly sins' will be used, in this series of small books, as a means for balancing healthy desires.

Each book will focus on one 'sin', it's corresponding....deity, kitchen herb, element, color, direction, day of the week, and Tarot Card. I've assigned meanings to each Card being used that are relevant for our purposes, if not traditional.

I've included instructions for circle casting, and for ritual. The ritual can be used for increasing or decreasing the influence of the 'sin' in yourself and in your Life.

CONTENTS.....

the first 3 'sins'....GREED, VANITY, & ENVY.

SATANIQUE MAGIQUE BOOK 1 GREED

GREED....

The desire for more than you have right now is a sign of a well person with healthy desires......just don't let wanting more keep you from enjoying and appreciating what you do have...it's foolish.

sin- GREED

kitchen herb- Cinnamon

deity- Satan

element- fire

color- red

direction-South

Tarot Card- XV The Devil

day of the week-Tuesday

you will need.....

-an image of Satan (statue, symbol, etc.)

-kitchen herb- Cinnamon

-one red candle

-the corresponding Tarot Card (XV)

-firesafe receptacle

-lighter

-altar

-altar cloth (optional)

-a comfortable chair

- charcoal

This can be done on a Tuesday or any time you feel the need. I've chosen Tuesday as we've now shaken off that Monday malaise and are ready to 'rock'.

Set everything in place so that you are facing South for this work (including the Tarot Card.....upright if increasing the influence of GREED, upside down if decreasing it)

next.............. - cast the circle clockwise if you wish to increase the influence of GREED,(in yourself or your Life) counter clockwise to decrease it.

1 casting a simple circle

-method one

- DRAW the circle around you and your workspace on the floor/ ground with chalk or by pouring salt....clockwise for positive (drawing in)work/counter clockwise for negative (banishing) work.

- while doing this FEEL the circle forming around you and your workspace.

-(I always envision a small doggie door for my Chihuahua to enter and exit through if he wishes)

-method two

- with a WAND, athame, your hand, or other(your choice)...while standing...DRAW the circle in the air around you and your workspace ....with your arm outstretched at just below shoulder height.........clockwise for positive (drawing in)work/counter clockwise for negative (banishing)work.

- while doing this FEEL the circle forming around you and your workspace.

-(I always envision a small doggie door for my Chihuahua to enter and exit through if he wishes)

2 taking down the circle (after ritual)

-method one

-SWEEP up the salt or chalk....moving around the circle in the direction opposite to that in which it was cast........FEEL the energy from the circle being absorbed into the Earth (even if you're several floors up in a building)

- dispose of the salt or chalk as you wish

-method two

- with a WAND, athame, your hand, or other(your choice)...while standing...ABSORB the energy from the circle in the air around you ....with your arm outstretched at just below shoulder height.......moving in the direction opposite to that which the circle was cast.

-store the item for later ritual use, if one was used.

RITUAL

Once the circle is cast.....

-ask Satan to join you in the circle

(skip this if you use a symbol, but don't actually work with deities)

-sprinkle the Cinnamon on the charcoal

-light the Cinnamon as an offering to Him (or just to help set the mood and to help you shift your consciousness)and speak a prayer to honor Him.

-light the red candle, and examine the Tarot Card (in the

chosen position..upright/increase or upside down/decrease)by it's light.

XV The Devil (card) MEANING...

UPRIGHT- self discipline, hard work, consious mind, focus, motivation, getting off your butt, doing the work needed, ask Satan to help you 'up your game' (or make an agreement with yourself to 'up your game')

UPSIDE DOWN- need to 'chill', relax your mind, go inward/ meditation/create art, etc, ask Satan to guide you in seeking fulfilment in areas other than career/wealth/obtaining (or make an agreement with yourself to do this), loosen up, lighten up, have some fun, let go

-sit and meditate with the card....take your time........allow your thoughts to form freely.......

-when through.....

-If you've invited Satan to join you and have asked for His assistance....Thank Him and bid Him farewell

-Thank the Tarot for sharing it's wisdom and beauty/for being a very useful tool

-EXTINGUISH all fires safely

-take down the circle in the opposite direction

-clean up

FINIS

CONTINUING THE WORK

If you've chosen to increase the influence of GREED in yourself and in your Life......when presented with desirable new opportunities say 'yes'.

Continue to look for ways to improve yourself and your sense of self worth......this comes about as a result of what you DO, not by what you think.

If you've chosen to decrease the influence of GREED in yourself and in your Life......when presented with extra work and opportunities.......learn to say 'no' when you can.

Look for ways to delegate work to others when possible (even if they won't do it EXACTLY as you would). Try letting go of control and take time to relax.

SATANIQUE MAGIQUE BOOK 2 VANITY

VANITY......

There's nothing wrong with feeling good about yourself...proud of your accomplishments...pleased with your appearance, but it's also important to appreciate the efforts of others which have benefited you.

sin- VANITY

kitchen herb- Sage

deity- Lucifer

element- air

color- yellow

direction- East

Tarot Card- XII The Hanged Man

day of the week-Saturday

you will need.....

-an image of Lucifer (statue, symbol, etc.)

-kitchen herb- Sage

-one yellow candle

-the corresponding Tarot Card (XII)

-firesafe receptacle

-lighter

-altar

-altar cloth (optional)

-a comfortable chair

- charcoal

This can be done on a Saturday or any time you feel the need. I've chosen Saturday as it's a popular night for going out to places where we can 'see and be seen'.......it's a chance to look our best and show off a bit, and have some fun.

Set everything in place so that you are facing East for this work (including the Tarot Card.....upright if increasing the influence of VANITY, upside down if decreasing it)

next............. - cast the circle clockwise if you wish to increase the influence of VANITY,(in yourself or your Life) counter clockwise to decrease it.

1 casting a simple circle

-method one

- DRAW the circle around you and your workspace on the floor/ ground with chalk or by pouring salt....clockwise for positive (drawing in)work/counter clockwise for negative (banishing) work.

- while doing this FEEL the circle forming around you and your workspace.

-(I always envision a small doggie door for my Chihuahua to enter and exit through if he wishes)

-method two

- with a WAND, athame, your hand, or other(your choice)...while standing...DRAW the circle in the air around you and your workspace ....with your arm outstretched at just below shoulder height.........clockwise for positive (drawing in)work/counter clockwise for negative (banishing)work.

- while doing this FEEL the circle forming around you and your workspace.

-(I always envision a small doggie door for my Chihuahua to enter and exit through if he wishes)

2 taking down the circle {after ritual}

-method one

-SWEEP up the salt or chalk....moving around the circle in the direction opposite to that in which it was cast........FEEL the energy from the circle being absorbed into the Earth (even if you're several floors up in a building)

- dispose of the salt or chalk as you wish

-method two

- with a WAND, athame, your hand, or other(your choice)...while standing...ABSORB the energy from the circle in the air around you ....with your arm outstretched at just below shoulder height.......moving in the direction opposite to that which the circle was cast.

-store the item for later ritual use, if one was used.

RITUAL

Once the circle is cast.....

-ask Lucifer to join you in the circle

(skip this if you use a symbol, but don't actually work with deities)

-sprinkle the Sage on the charcoal

-light the Sage as an offering to Him (or just to help set the mood and to help you shift your consciousness)and speak a prayer to honor Him.

-light the yellow candle, and examine the Tarot Card (in the chosen position..upright/increase or upside down/decrease)by it's light.

XII The Hanged Man (card) MEANING...

UPRIGHT- sacrifice for the attainment of knowledge, physical beauty, increased strength, agility-mental and/or physical... ask Lucifer to help you enjoy profitable self imposed sacrifice (or make an agreement with yourself to enjoy it)

UPSIDE DOWN- need to lighten up, not take you or anything (unprofitably) seriously, take time to relax- to laugh... ask Lucifer to guide you in seeking joy in areas other than in increasing knowledge and beauty (or make an agreement with yourself to do this), loosen up, have some fun, let go

-sit and meditate with the card....take your time........allow your thoughts to form freely.......

-when through.....

-If you've invited Lucifer to join you and have asked for His assistance....Thank Him and bid Him farewell

-Thank the Tarot for sharing it's wisdom and beauty/for being a very useful tool

-EXTINGUISH all fires safely

-take down the circle in the opposite direction

-clean up

FINIS

CONTINUING THE WORK

If you've chosen to increase the influence of VANITY in yourself and in your Life......when presented with desirable new opportunities for self improvement say 'yes'.

Continue to look for ways to improve yourself, body & mind.

If you've chosen to decrease the influence of VANITY

in yourself and in your Life......when presented with challenging ways to improve yourself unnecessarily.......learn to say 'no'.

Look for ways to value and appreciate the progress you've made and will continue to make at a pace that is right for you and your true desires....and the vision you have for you at your personal best.

SATANIQUE MAGIQUE BOOK 3 ENVY

ENVY....

Envy can be a great motivator. When someone has something I want ....I can feel inspired to work to get it for myself as well. As long as I don't use it to feel sorry for myself or to resent others for what they have worked for (or have been given-none of my business really) it can be truly beneficial.

sin- ENVY

kitchen herb- dried BASIL

deity- HECATE

element- Earth plane/planet

color- green

direction-center

Tarot Card- III The Empress

day of the week-Thursday

you will need.....

-an image of Hecate (statue, symbol, etc.)

-kitchen herb- Basil

-one green candle

-the corresponding Tarot Card (III)

-firesafe receptacle

-lighter

-altar

-altar cloth (optional)

-a comfortable chair

- charcoal

This can be done on a Thursday or any time you feel the need. I've chosen Thursday as it is the day of the week that feels the most grounded to me......we've gotten over the Wednesday hump, but haven't hit the excitement of Friday or the anticipation of the weekend yet.

Set everything in place in a circular pattern on your altar, (including the Tarot Card.....upright if increasing the influence of ENVY, upside down if decreasing it) face any direction you like for this work

next............. - cast the circle clockwise if you wish to increase the influence of ENVY,(in yourself or your Life) counter clockwise to decrease it.

1 casting a simple circle

-method one

- DRAW the circle around you and your workspace on the floor/ ground with chalk or by pouring salt....clockwise for positive (drawing in)work/counter clockwise for negative (banishing) work.

- while doing this FEEL the circle forming around you and your workspace.

-(I always envision a small doggie door for my Chihuahua to enter and exit through if he wishes)

-method two

- with a WAND, athame, your hand, or other(your choice)...while standing...DRAW the circle in the air around you and your workspace ....with your arm outstretched at just below shoulder height.........clockwise for positive (drawing in)work/counter clockwise for negative (banishing)work.

- while doing this FEEL the circle forming around you and your workspace.

-(I always envision a small doggie door for my Chihuahua to enter and exit through if he wishes)

2 taking down the circle {after ritual}

-method one

-SWEEP up the salt or chalk....moving around the circle in the direction opposite to that in which it was cast.......FEEL the energy from the circle being absorbed into the Earth (even if you're several floors up in a building)

- dispose of the salt or chalk as you wish

-method two

- with a WAND, athame, your hand, or other(your choice)...while standing...ABSORB the energy from the circle in the air around you ....with your arm outstretched at just below shoulder height.......moving in the direction opposite to that which the circle was cast.

-store the item for later ritual use, if one was used.

RITUAL

Once the circle is cast.....

-ask Hecate to join you in the circle

(skip this if you use a symbol, but don't actually work with deities)

-sprinkle the Basil on the charcoal

-light the Basil as an offering to Her (or just to help set the mood and to help you shift your consciousness)and speak a prayer to honor Her.

-light the green candle, and examine the Tarot Card (in the chosen position..upright/increase or upside down/decrease)by it's light.

III The Empress (card) MEANING...

UPRIGHT- Bounty, fertility, plush landscape, land of plenty, growth, attainment... ask Hecate to help you go out and get what you truly desire, and to leave behind any doubt in your abilities or worth.

UPSIDE DOWN- pause of growth, attainment, etc.... ask Hecate to help you focus on what's 'good' in your Life rather than what's lacking, take time to appreciate what you do have...remind your-self of those who have less than you.

-sit and meditate with the card....take your time........allow your thoughts to form freely.......

-when through.....

-If you've invited Hecate to join you and have asked for Her as-sistance....Thank Her and bid Her farewell

-Thank the Tarot for sharing it's wisdom and beauty/for being a very useful tool

-EXTINGUISH all fires safely

-take down the circle in the opposite direction

-clean up

FINIS

CONTINUING THE WORK

If you've chosen to increase the influence of ENVY in yourself and in your Life......when presented with desirable new opportunities to get more of what you want, whether it be tangile objects or intangibles...go for it, let ENVY inspire you to break out of your 'comfort zone'.

Continue to look for new ways to get what you admire in others for yourself.

If you've chosen to decrease the influence of ENVY

in yourself and in your Life.....continue to be grateful for what you do have, find ways to make what you already have useful again. Renew your enthusiasm for the familiar. Take pride in what you've already earned/acheived.

When comparing yourself to others...focus on those who have less.....material success, education, experience, etc......not to be shitty, but to gage your personal success.

About me.....

I was raised Catholic, but knew it wasn't a proper fit for me at an early age. The idea of confession made no sense to me and I felt no reasonable motivation for sharing my private thoughts with members of the clergy, nor did I appreciate others imposing their beliefs and rules on me.

As an adult...I've worked with the Tarot for 30 years, and have read professionally for clients on ebay and in the shop I ran for a number of years in the 'real world' with my spouse, Andrew.

I was a practicing Pagan for 13 years and was a member of "The Church of the Three Witches", a collective of (Wiccan) Solitary Practitioners who would get together for outdoor rituals on Solar and Lunar occasions, in Philadelphia, Pa.

I discovered Satanism in 2010 and have practiced Spiritual Satanism since.

I have explored Atheistic, Theistic and Spiritual approaches to Satan, Satanism and Satanic philosophy... and am a member of "The Satanic Temple".

I am always exploring and have learned and hope to continue to learn.....from many different paths and philosophies.

other books by the author.....

The Wheel of the Year, Kitschy Archetypes & Real Deities, Devil's HALLOWEEN ANYTIME Tree of Sobriety JOURNAL, Yule Be Fine, HELLthy QUEER Creating, Satanique Magique book 1- GREED, Satanique Magique book 2-VANITY, and Satanique Magique book 3-ENVY

HELLthy QUEER CREATING

Sigils for Empowerment

David Byron Rivera 2020

Dedication

I dedicate this book to anyone who has been told that they are not the master of their sex and body, and to anyone who has been exposed to an oppressive indoctrination, religious or not.

CONTENTS

1 casting a simple circle

-method one

- DRAW the circle around you and your workspace on the floor/ground with chalk or by pouring salt....clockwise for positive (drawing in)work/counter clockwise for negative (banishing) work.

- while doing this FEEL the circle forming around you and your workspace.

-(I always envision a small doggie door for my Chihuahua to enter and exit through if he wishes)

-method two

- with a WAND, athame, your hand, or other(your choice)...while standing...DRAW the circle in the air around you and your workspace ....with your arm outstretched at just below shoulder height.........clockwise for positive (drawing in)work/counter clockwise for negative (banishing)work.

- while doing this FEEL the circle forming around you and your workspace.

-(I always envision a small doggie door for my Chihuahua to enter and exit through if he wishes)

2 taking down the circle (after ritual)

-method one

-SWEEP up the salt or chalk....moving around the circle in the direction opposite to that in which it was cast.......FEEL the energy from the circle being absorbed into the Earth (even if you're several floors up in a building)

- dispose of the salt or chalk as you wish

-method two

- with a WAND, athame, your hand, or other(your choice)...while standing...ABSORB the energy from the circle in the air around you ....with your arm outstretched at just below shoulder height.......moving in the direction opposite to that which the circle was cast.

-store the item for later ritual use, if one was used.

3 purification of the self

Before you celebrate what makes you ...uniquely you .....you need to banish unhealthy thoughts and influences. Whether they stem from a religious upbringing or from any other beliefs that make you feel 'wrong'... they have to be cleared away to make room for the positive.

(This can be done before ritual, or anytime you feel the need)

you will need:

-a symbol of the belief or belief system drawn on a piece of paper.

-a black candle

-your favorite incense (optional)

-altar or work space

-lighter or matches

-a firesafe vessel

-a comfortable chair

-an object to represent healthy self pride (a picture of you or an award you've won, etc)

-Set up your materials and workspace

-cast a simple circle

-light the incense (if you've elected to use it), or just enjoy the scent of it

-sit and focus on your symbol and the pain the belief(s) attached to it have caused you ....take your time..........allow yourself to really feel it.

-once you feel ready to release it...light the candle and burn the symbol in it's flame and toss it into the vessel....let it burn completely.

-when through.......extinguish any remaining fires safely.

-take down the circle

-clean up

FINIS

4 PAN- for our purposes this half goat/half man Greek deity is being honored in relation to sexual orientation.

His Tarot Card is.. XV The Devil (in some decks He is actually represented as Pan).

YOU WILL NEED

-paper, wood, clay, etc (your choice-for creating your sigil)

-paints, markers, etc (your choice-for creating your sigil)

-salt or a wand for circle casting

-Tarot Card -Major Arcana XV (to be placed in the center of the altar)

-this book

-altar or workspace

-a comfortable seat

-a representation of the earth element (a potted plant, reversed pentacle, etc)

- a brown candle to honour Pan

- a lighter or matches

- any additional items you'd like to incorporate

-a firesafe receptacle for any dicarded matches, etc (please use all precautions)

-SET UP EVERYTHING BEING USED FOR THE RITUAL

-CAST A SIMPLE CIRCLE

-LIGHT THE BROWN CANDLE, and any incense (optional), IN HONOR OF PAN

-RECITE:

I honor you Pan, god of sexuality,

god of free expression

I know, through you, that ALL that occurs in Nature is natural

and I am of the Natural World

All Hail Pan!!

-TAKE A FEW MINUTES TO CLOSE YOUR EYES AND RELAX YOUR BREATHING

-WHEN READY......OPEN YOUR EYES

CREATE a sigil for- your personal expression of your sexual orientation(s).

This can be as simple or complex as you wish, it is uniquely personal.

Use your paper, clay, etc......and markers, paint, etc..to make something you'd like to use for future work or meditation.

While working, think about any other animals (humans are mammals) that express a variety of orientations.....gay, straight, bisexual, asexual, etc..

when through....

CHARGE the sigil by envisioning it growing from a tree like a piece of fruit and being illuminated by the Sun, every line being filled with bright glowing Sunlight.

After enjoying this for awhile...

-extinguish any fires

-take down the circle

-store your sigil somewhere safe

-clean up

FINIS

5 LOKI- for our purposes this gender shifting Norse deity is being honored in relation to the expression of gender(s).

Loki's Tarot Card is.. 0 The Fool (usually depicted as a gender-neutral figure)

YOU WILL NEED

-paper, wood, clay, etc (your choice-for creating your sigil)

-paints, markers, etc (your choice-for creating your sigil)

-salt or a wand for circle casting

-Tarot Card -Major Arcana 0 (to be place in the center of the altar)

-this book

-altar or workspace

-a comfortable seat

-a representation of the air element (a feather, dagger, etc)

- a yellow candle to honour Loki

- a lighter or matches

- any additional items you'd like to incorporate

-a firesafe receptacle for any dicarded matches, etc (please use all precautions)

-SET UP EVERYTHING BEING USED FOR THE RITUAL

-CAST A SIMPLE CIRCLE

-LIGHT THE YELLOW CANDLE, and any incense (optional), IN HONOR OF LOKI

-RECITE:

I honor you Loki, deity of mutable gender,

deity of free expression

I know, through you, that I am free to be my true self. I know gender does not always remain fixed in Nature

and I am of the Natural World

All Hail Loki!!

-TAKE A FEW MINUTES TO CLOSE YOUR EYES AND RELAX YOUR BREATHING

-WHEN READY......OPEN YOUR EYES

CREATE a sigil for- your personal expression of your gender(s).

This can be as simple or complex as you wish, it is uniquely personal.

Use your paper, clay, etc.....and markers, paint, etc..to make something you'd like to use for future work or meditation.

While working, think about any other animals (humans are mammals) that can alter their expession of gender(s)

when through....

CHARGE the sigil by envisioning it gently falling from the night sky illuminated by the Moon, every line being filled with bright glowing Moonlight.

After enjoying this for awhile...

-extinguish any fires

-take down the circle

-store your sigil somewhere safe

-clean up

FINIS

Notes....

____
____
____
____
____

25

www.ingramcontent.com/pod-product-compliance
Lightning Source LLC
Chambersburg PA
CBHW051944150726
47999CB00006B/2356